LILLENAS®

Imagine That

Creative
and
Interactive
Ideas
for
Teaching
Kids
the Bible

by Jeff Smith

Lillenas PUBLISHING COMPANY

KANSAS CITY, MO 64141

Questions? Please write or call:
Lillenas Publishing Company
Drama Resources
P.O. Box 419527
Kansas City, MO 64141
Phone: 816-931-1900 ● Fax: 816-412-8390
E-mail: drama@lillenas.com
Web: www.lillenas.com/drama

Cover art by Michael Walsh

Dedication

A friend tells the story of how her young son would bound into the middle of her daily grind with unbridled joy to report that a train was passing by a few blocks away. If for no reason than to appease his unfettered enthusiasm, she pauses to share his small treasure before he runs away to conquer another faraway land. But the lingering sound of the train rolling down a distant track is a haunting reminder that time with our children passes by much too quickly. "My son," she said, "helped me to hear the trains again." When she told me the story, I resolved to try to be a better listener. Do you know what I heard? Train whistles. It's hard to tell if they are coming or going, but the sound of trains passing by is all around us. They have become my call to prayer. I pray for my children and their salvation. I also pray that I will be wise enough to know when to lead them and when to follow them. It's funny what you hear when you're listening. Are you listening now?

> People have said to me all of my life,
> "Kids grow up fast."
> And it cuts like a knife, hurts like a sting
> It tugs and it pulls on the ol' heart strings.
> So enjoy every day before they're past.

(From "I Can Hear the Trains Again," by Jeffrey C. Smith on the album *Revelations* © 1998.)

To my precious children, Ben and Samuel.
Thank you for helping me hear the trains again.

Contents

Preface

As I write the introduction to this book, a staggering thought jumps into my head. What makes me think I'm qualified to write a book like this? So, I start to muster some credentials together and the best I can do is this: I was one and I have two. The former qualification may be a little outdated (never mind how much), but the latter is very current. Our house is often a school that teaches us how to be more effective in communicating with children. Additionally, the need to impact the lives of children for the sake of the gospel has never been greater.

Another qualification may be that I have worked with some very effective children's ministries. They are the programs where children are dragging their parents to church. They are effective, in part, because their ministry is relevant to the children and the culture they live in. They use computers and interactive games, video clips, visual teaching techniques, contemporary music, resource centers, and a host of other creative and contemporary teaching tools. Relevance is important. Allegory, parody, imitation, reference, innuendo, and story are all ways to connect the kingdom of God to the culture.

That's what Jesus did! He made the kingdom of God relevant. When He was in a field, He would talk about the kingdom of God being like a man who went out to sow his seeds. When He was in a vineyard, He would include a story about a certain man who owned a vineyard. When He preached the Sermon on the Mount, I believe He used illustrations, props, landmarks, references, and even acted out some of His messages. Can't you see Him picking up a stick and referencing a nearby log when He talked about the hypocrite who judges his brother? The log, the stick, the setting, the cultural icon are all what I like to refer to as "sanctified bait." It's the idea of making whatever is available a hook or tool to help people understand what the kingdom of God is like.

I don't like to quote statistics. Facts don't always point to the truth. Still, it is widely recognized that people don't learn or retain what they learn by listening. The advent of television has made us more visually dependent. Additionally, the information age is teaching us to learn by interacting. I am not insinuating that we need to change the Word of God. But the Logos Word has more dimension than just the written words on a page. The text has context that gives it texture and depth. Not only are they the words of life, but they are alive and, consequently, should be lively. This book is a collection of ideas to illustrate and involve kids in the process of learning the gospel. These concepts are not necessarily new or cutting edge to some children's ministries. Still, you might find a clever twist or a unique approach or application to an old idea. Hopefully, you will find bigger ideas like these between the lines and the pages of this book:

1. **Aim high.** I think it's a travesty that we water down our approach to sharing the gospel when it comes to children. Generally, we aim so low that we end up shooting ourselves in the foot. Truth is always truth and recog-

nizable in the form of a clever story, good dramatization, or fun song. What I want to say about being creative with children is the same thing I want to say about being creative in general. I don't draw a different line in the sand for children. I learned this from the theatre. It may be more an issue of appropriateness, but a good children's play is a good play. When I started my ministry in 1987, the Lord spoke a word to my spirit about the nature of what it was I would be doing. Basically, it was to watch people watch the Word come to life. I have been watching ever since and can tell you that I'm always amazed at how the four-year-old will sit on the lap of the father next to the grandmother and they are all captivated by the dramatic portrayal of the blind man in John 9. Dramatizations of God's Word should be riveting.

2. **Good ideas breed good ideas.** Maybe another way to say it would be "Build the field and they will come." A good book on a subject like this should spawn more ideas. In a sense, I wanted to build a field, turn on the lights, and see who would come out to play. You will never learn how to be more creative in your approach to anything by reading a manual or how-to book. You must experience the process in order to learn anything about creativity. Only to the degree that you lose your sense of wonder will you be hindered in the creative possibilities of sharing God's Word.

3. **Adopt a new perspective.** I'm not wired the same way as most. (Did someone say "Amen"? Did I get a witness?) So, this point may be biased. But I would encourage you to look for the sacred in the secular and the extraordinary in the ordinary. I try to find God in the world around me; not only in the inexpressible beauty of His creation but also in the creations of humankind. I can find Him in a book, a play, in my son's school, in a crowded mall, in a country-and-western song (rarely!). George Lucas may not believe in God, but I could see good versus evil in *Star Wars*. Stephen King doesn't believe in organized religion, but I can find elements of the Christian walk in some of his stories. I can listen to some secular music and turn it into a worship song. Not all artists fashion art that is redemptive. Still, my point is that if you're looking for God, you can find Him in the strangest places. I've written a little ditty called "The Cereal Song," which talks about hearing the voice of God on aisle four of the local grocery store.

> *The evidence seemed quite surreal*
> *To talk to God about cereal*
> *But He spoke with others long before*
> *In stranger spots than grocery stores.*

(From "The Cereal Song," written by Jeffrey C. Smith, © 1999.)

Finding new ways to tell the "Old Story" doesn't have to be difficult. Actually, I believe it should be fun. Perhaps we need to be more like children in order to teach them. Perhaps we need to approach the telling of these great stories and unchanging truths with the wonder and amazement we had when we first heard them as children, but with a greater sense of the world that children live in today. Regarding possibilities, there are far more apples in the seed than seeds in the apple. John's last statement in his Gospel account is, "If every one of them [the things Jesus did] were written down, I suppose that even the whole world would not have room for the books that would be written." I guess we'll run out of paper before we run out of ideas.

Object Lessons

Object lessons are an excellent way to turn common, ordinary items into vehicles to tell Bible stories. I like to play a common improvisation game that requires an actor to use an item as a prop in a way it was not intended. For example, a hat can become a bowl or a Frisbee or a steering wheel or whatever the improvisation may require. A credit card can become a slice of bread, a camera, or a patch over your eye. The following ideas—"Pumpkin Time," "The Rumor Box," "Good Things," and "Tool Story"—all capitalize, to some degree, on making the ordinary . . . extraordinary.

Pumpkin Time

Scripture Reference: "If we confess our sins, he is faithful and just and will forgive us our sins and purify us from all unrighteousness" (1 John 1:9).

What You Need:
- Two pumpkins
- Paring knife
- Candle
- Matches
- Flashlight
- Tongue depressor (optional)

(Make sure the paring knife and the matches stay out of reach at all times.)

What You Need to Make:
- Cut out a "lid" for one pumpkin.
- For the second pumpkin, cut the lid and clean out the "guts" of the pumpkin. Carve out two eyes and a nose, but no mouth.

What You Need to Say *(before you begin, take time to relate a safety message about the knife and the matches):* The Bible says that there is nothing good in us (Romans 3:11-12). I know that God's Word is true, but I wanted to see for myself if I could find just one good thing. *(Pick a child and tell him or her that you want to check down his or her throat to see if you can find one good thing down there. Have the child open his or her mouth and use the tongue depressor and flashlight as if you were a doctor looking for a throat infection.)* Was the Bible talking about something that we could see? What is in us that is so bad? [Sin] The Bible says that all have sinned and fallen short of the glory of God (Romans 3:23). Sin makes us feel "yucky," like the inside of this pumpkin. *(Lift the lid of the pumpkin, which has not been gutted, and let the kids reach down into the pumpkin to feel it.)* But if we pray to Jesus, He will make us clean (1 John 1:9). *(Take the second pumpkin that is cleaned out and lift the lid for the children to look inside.)* Do you know something else? Not only does Jesus make us clean, but He replaces the sin with a light . . . the light of His Holy Spirit to help us to do good things. *(Light the candle and place it inside the pumpkin. Put the lid back on the pumpkin and let all the children look at it. If it is dark outside, you can turn off the lights or go outside and look at it.)* What is missing on the pumpkin's face? *(They may have already mentioned this before now.)* I know. *(Blow out the light, remove the candle, and carve out a smile on the pumpkin's face. Then restore the light.)* When we ask Jesus to take away our sin, He cleans us up on the inside and then puts the light of His Holy Spirit in our heart to help us to do good things. That makes everyone happy.

(As an optional ending you can roast and salt the pumpkin seeds and serve them as a snack. You might also pass out the seeds as a reminder of the lesson. If you're really ambitious, you can make a pumpkin pie and serve it as a snack.)

The Rumor Box

Scripture Reference: "You shall not give false testimony against your neighbor" (Exodus 20:16).

What You Need:
- A rectangular box no smaller than 12" deep, 10" to 12" wide, and 18" to 20" long.
- Two items that are similar in nature but different in size. Examples would be:
- a golf ball and a baseball (i.e., two balls)
- a tissue and a handkerchief
- small glasses (sunglasses) (doll, toy, etc.) and regular or oversized glasses (sunglasses)
- a 4- to 6-ounce paper cup and a 12- to 16-ounce paper cup
- a dictionary and a Bible (The dictionary should be bigger than the Bible.)

What You Need to Make:
- Cut a hole on each end of the box. Make it big enough to put your hand through and pull out any of the objects listed above. Wrap the box in an attractive wrapping paper. Attach a drape or piece of fabric on the inside of each hole so that you cannot look into the box but are still be able to put your hand into it.
- Place the larger of each object inside the box and replace the lid.

What You Need to Say: Come and see my very special box. Look what I can do with it. *(Take one of the smaller objects such as the cup and place it in the box through the hole. Reach into the box with the other hand and through the opposite hole and pull out the larger cup.)* Wow, it's my new invention and I'm going to be rich! Let's see what else I can do with this box. *(Repeat this action with some of your other props.)* Isn't this great? What shall I call it? *(Let the children pick out some names.)* Those are all great ideas. What do you think about calling it a rumor box? Do you know what a rumor is? It is a story or statement that may not be true. Sometimes it can be an exaggeration or even a lie about someone else. People start a rumor by saying things like, "Well I heard that so-and-so did this and that," or "Did you hear that so-and-so did this and that?" Well just think of how big the lie can get if we keep spreading rumors. *(Put a piece of string into the rumor box and pull out a rope or put in a tissue and pull out a sheet! Show the children a dictionary.)* Boys and girls, do you know what this is? A dictionary is full of words and their meanings. We should be careful what we say about people. *(Put the dictionary through the "bigger" end of the rumor box and pull out a Bible from the "smaller" end.)* The Bible says, "My mouth speaks what is true, for my lips detest wickedness" (Proverbs 8:7). Remember that bigger isn't always better; especially if it's words that aren't the truth.

Good Things

Scripture Reference: "In all things God works for the good of those who love him, who have been called according to his purpose" (Romans 8:28).

What You Need:
- 2 eggs
- a bottle of cooking oil
- a bag of flour
- a box of baking soda

What You Need to Make:
- a cake

What You Need to Say *(Ask the kids if they would like to have something really good to eat. From a nearby grocery bag, pull out two eggs and offer them to the kids to eat. [Hopefully, they will not want to eat the eggs raw!] Then pull out a bottle of cooking oil and ask them if they would like to have some of the cooking oil instead. Do the same with the bag of flour and the box of baking soda. Try and seem confused about the fact that the children don't like any of these ingredients. Try to get them to say something to the effect that these items don't taste very good. Once you have established this, pull out a cake from your bag and tell them that all these items; eggs, cooking oil, flour, and baking soda, are some of the ingredients in a cake. Explain to the children that sometimes things happen to us that we don't like. They are like ingredients that don't taste good. But Romans 8:28 says, "In all things God works for the good of those who love him, who have been called according to his purpose." We should trust God to take care of us, even when things happen to us that make us sad. Just like some of the ingredients of a cake don't taste good by themselves, they can be used with other things to make something wonderful in our lives. If appropriate, have the kids repeat the scripture verse and then slice the cake and offer pieces to them.)*

Tool Story

Scripture Reference: "If you confess with your mouth, 'Jesus is Lord,' and believe in your heart that God raised him from the dead, you will be saved" (Romans 10:9).

What You Need: You will need the following props in a toolbox: plane, tape measure, level, drill, drill bit, crowbar (lever), pliers (or grips or snips), nut, bolt, wood screw, saw, vice, hammer, nail, washer, carpenter's ruler, wrench, ruler, socket, plumb line

What You Need to Do: As you begin to tell this story, open the toolbox and pull out the tool listed in italics. Again, if you are with an older group, you might want to pull out the prop and let them call out the name of the tool as if they were telling part of the story.

What You Need to Say: This is the story of Jesus, a master builder. Born in Bethlehem, He grew up in Nazareth, where His father, Joseph, taught Him the tools of the trade. They say He was PLANE *[plane]* to look at by any MEASURE *[tape measure]*. Like other boys His age, He was well schooled in Jewish religion, DRILLED *[drill]* in the ways of the Torah. He was LEVELHEADED *[level]*, but A LITTLE BIT *[drill bit]* angry at how the religious leaders used the Law as LEVERAGE *[crowbar]* to hold the people in their GRIPS *[pliers or grips]*. Jesus told the people about God's grace and how much He loved them. This made the religious leaders NUTS *[nut]*, and they would BOLT *[bolt]* back to their meetings and WOULD SCREWTINIZE *[wood screw]* ways to kill Jesus. But Jesus wasn't afraid of them. He SAW *[saw]* how VICE *[vice]* and sin made the people WRETCHED *[wrench]* and knew that only the truth about God would set them free. When the people started to claim that Jesus should be their RULER *[ruler]*, the religious leaders decided to SOCK IT *[socket]* to Jesus by PLUMB LYIN' *[plumb line]* about things that He said and did. They HAMMERED *[hammer]* Him with questions in a mockery of a trial and finally NAILED *[nail]* Him when He told them that He was the Son of God. They hung Him on a wooden cross *(make a cross with the carpenter's ruler)* and He died. They took His dead body and put Him in a tomb. *(Close the lid to the empty toolbox.)* But three days later, the stone was rolled away and Jesus' body wasn't there. *(Open the toolbox and show them it's empty.)* That's because Jesus is alive again. He took all the tools His Heavenly Father gave Him to use and He built a bridge. *(Unfold the carpenter's ruler out of the cross into a straight line.)* It is a bridge that leads us back to God. *(Return the carpenter's ruler to the cross.)* Would you like to CROSS the bridge? *(This is a great place to share the plan of salvation and lead the children in a sinner's prayer if appropriate.)* Remember, God has given us all the TOOLS we need to be master builders too.

Silly Songs and Parodies

Music is a powerful tool of communication. How many of us can reach back into our memories and pull out lyrics to songs we sang years ago? My grandmother, who is still living at the time of this writing, is in the advanced stages of Alzheimer's disease. Still, she can remember most of the words to traditional hymns. To that end, music is often used as a teaching tool. I will often make up parodies using contemporary music as a way to capture the attention of an audience. In a way, it's closely related to the concept of an object lesson, but the object is a song. I have chosen some fairly juvenile, recognizable songs from the public domain to demonstrate how easy it is to incorporate silly songs or parodies into your repertoire. Also, consider using finger puppets, stick puppets, flannel board pictures, or just simple pantomime to act out the story while it is being sung. Once you have considered these ideas, perhaps you could come up with your own ideas to simple songs like "Row Your Boat," "She'll Be Comin' Round the Mountain," or "Home on the Range."

I Heard the Voice of the Father

(to the tune of "Alleluia")

(This simple ditty gets small children involved with sounds and hand movements. This piece works well with the story of 1 Samuel 3. There are several variations of the idea listed here. Feel free to add your own or delete these suggestions as needed.)

I heard the sound of the Father singing,
I heard the sound of the Father say,
"Watcha gonna do, Watcha gonna do, children,"
"Watcha gonna do when I call . . . call your name?"

(Add clapping.) I heard the sound of the Father clapping,
I heard the sound of the Father say,
"Watcha gonna do, Watcha gonna do, children,"
"Watcha gonna do when I call . . . call your name?"

(Snap your fingers.) I heard the sound of the Father snapping,
I heard the sound of the Father say . . .

(Speak like a rap.) I heard the sound of the Father rapping,
I heard the sound of the Father say . . .

(Shout) I heard the sound of the Father shouting,
I heard the sound of the Father say . . .

(Whisper) I heard the sound of the Father whisper,
I heard the sound of the Father say . . .

(Laugh) I heard the sound of the Father laughing,
I heard the sound of the Father say . . .

Babel

(to the tune of "B-I-N-G-O")

(Remember the old song about a dog named Bingo? Each time the song was re-peated another letter of the dog's name, which was spelled out in the song, was dropped and replaced with silence, clapping, or another sound. In this adaptation, each letter in the word "babel" is replaced with the sound "blah." As the story un-folds and the song goes on, it sounds more ridiculous.)

There was a tower made by man
And Babel was its name, oh,
B-a-b-e-l, B-a-b-e-l, B-a-b-e-l
And Babel was its name, oh.

There was tower built so high
And Babel was its name, oh,
(Blah) a-b-e-l, *(Blah)* a-b-e-l, *(Blah)* a-b-e-l
And Babel was its name, oh.

There was a tower [that] touched the sky
And Babel was its name, oh,
(Blah) (Blah) b-e-l, *(Blah) (Blah)* b-e-l, *(Blah) (Blah)* b-e-l
And Babel was its name, oh.

There was a tower [that] made God sad
And Babel was its name, oh,
(Blah) (Blah) (Blah) e-l, *(Blah) (Blah) (Blah)* e-l, *(Blah) (Blah) (Blah)* e-l
And Babel was its name, oh.

There was a tower [that] made God mad
And Babel was its name, oh,
(Blah) (Blah) (Blah) (Blah)-l, *(Blah) (Blah) (Blah) (Blah)*-l, *(Blah) (Blah) (Blah)*
    (Blah)-l
And Babel was its name, oh.

God gave man a funny gift
And Babel was its name, oh,
(Blah) (Blah) (Blah) (Blah) (Blah), (Blah) (Blah) (Blah) (Blah) (Blah), (Blah) (Blah)
    (Blah) (Blah) (Blah)
And Babel was its name, oh.

Abraham
(to the tune of "This Ol' Man")

(This is another great children's song that can be used to teach a Bible story. I recommend that a chorus leader sing the verses and the children join in on the chorus. A simple set of hand gestures or movements can be added to the chorus.)

This ol' man, Abraham,
Loved his God the great I AM.

(Add children.) With a knick-knack paddywhack,
Learning to obey, trusting God in every way.

This ol' man had a boy,
Named him Isaac, what a joy.
(Chorus)

This ol' man's son would grow
Strong and handsome, don't you know?
(Chorus)

This ol' man heard God's plea
What do you love more than Me?
(Chorus)

This ol' man made a choice,
Listened to Jehovah's voice.
(Chorus)

This ol' man raised his knife,
Trusted God with Isaac's life.
(Chorus)

This ol' man's great reward,
Made a promise with his Lord.
(Chorus)

God was pleased, sent a ram,
That's the story of Abraham.
(Chorus)

Gaming

Games are another way to tell Bible stories that don't require you to "reinvent the wheel" in order to be creative in your approach to teaching. There are many children's games like red rover or ring-around-a-rosy or tag that can be slightly adapted to make a story in the Bible seem more relevant. I have chosen three recognizable games, Marco Polo, button, button, who has the button? and musical chairs to teach Bible truths.

Marco Polo
(The Lost Sheep)

(Read John 10:11-18, 27. One person is the SHEPHERD. *They are blindfolded and put in the middle of the room. The other children scatter around the room. When the* SHEPHERD *calls for the sheep [decide on a word like "obey" or "trust" or the verse "My sheep know my voice and they obey"] the children respond by bleating the name "Jesus." The* SHEPHERD *uses the voice of the children to "lead" him around the room. You can decide if the children [sheep] can move around the room or stand still. When the* SHEPHERD *touches the sheep, they are "found" and move to the pen where they are "safe." The children should take turns being the* SHEPHERD.)

Musical Chairs
(The Parable of the Unmerciful Servant)

(Read the parable of the unmerciful servant in Matthew 18:23-35. This is a movement exercise to reinforce the circular, moving nature of forgiveness. Have all the kids sit in chairs in a circle.)

Assign the Following Movements:

"OUTSTANDING"—Stand up

"MARCH"—March in place

"FORGIVE/FORGIVENESS/FORGIVEN/etc."—Alternate walking around the
circle and sitting on a chair *(i.e., The first time I say "forgive" in the story,
everyone moves in a clockwise direction. The next time I use the word "forgive" or any derivative like "forgiveness," stop quickly and sit in a chair as fast
as you can. After each scramble for a seat, at least one or more chairs will be
taken out of the circle.)*

NARRATOR: Once there was a king. He was an OUTSTANDING king. One day
he was MARCHING around his throne deciding if he should show FORGIVENESS to a servant who owed him a lot of money.

(Remove a chair.)

He called for the servant and demanded complete payment of the
debt or he would throw him and all his family into jail. The servant groveled and begged and pleaded. Oh please, mighty king, have mercy upon
me and grant me your FORGIVENESS. *(Pause)*

The OUTSTANDING king MARCHED over to the servant and seeing
his pitiful state had mercy and granted him FORGIVENESS.

(Remove a chair.)

The servant was overjoyed and went running out into the streets
telling everyone how the kind the king had been to grant his FORGIVENESS. *(Pause)*

While running around outside, he saw, OUTSTANDING in the
streets, a man who owed him some money. He MARCHED right over to
the man, suddenly forgetting about the FORGIVENESS that he had received from the king.

(Remove a chair.)

He started choking the man, demanding payment of the debt or he
would have that man and his family thrown into prison until the debt
could be paid in full. The poor, pitiful man begged and pleaded for FORGIVENESS. *(Pause)*

But the man would show him none and had the poor fellow thrown
into prison. Some OUTSTANDING citizens in the community saw what
happened and were outraged! They MARCHED to the king's palace to inform the king what happened. Of course, the king who had shown FORGIVENESS to the servant was outraged.

(Remove a chair.)

Could it be that this servant on whom I had such great compassion and mercy would go out and not show FORGIVENESS to his brother? *(Pause)*

And so the king called for his guards who were OUTSTANDING in the hallway and told them to MARCH right out and bring that UNFOR-GIVING servant back to him.

(Remove a chair.)

The guards looked everywhere for the servant but could not find him because he had heard how mad the king was at him for not FOR-GIVING his fellow servant. *(Pause)*

Eventually, the guards found the man OUTSTANDING in a cave and they MARCHED him right back to the king. The king was furious with the servant. You despicable, worthless servant. I showed you FORGIVE-NESS.

(Remove a chair.)

And then you couldn't FORGIVE your fellow servant?

The OUTSTANDING king ordered the guards to MARCH him down to the prison and torture him until he could pay back all that he owed. For anyone who won't show FORGIVENESS to his brother.

(Remove a chair.)

Will not be FORGIVEN.

(NOTE: If there is a large group, you can repeat the story FASTER or you can take out more chairs between the movements.)

Button, Button, Who Has the Button?

(Giving)

(Read 2 Corinthians 9:7. This old, old game can be used as a way to teach the importance of a cheerful giver. Sit the children around the room in a circle. As the "leader," you will place a button between the palms of your hands and put your hands together in a prayerlike posture. You will instruct the children in the circle to do the same. Then, you will pass your hands between, but not through, the hands of each child in the circle. At one point, you will drop the button into the hands of one of the children without acknowledging that you have slipped the button in the child's hand. After you have made your way around the circle, you ask the question, "Button, button, who has the button?" Go around the circle and ask the children one by one to guess who has the button. The first person that guesses correctly gets to be the leader for the next pass. The person who has been given the button should guess someone else in order to fool the children. Talk about the story of the widow's offering in Luke 21:1-4 and then play the game again. Mention 2 Corinthians 9:7, "Each man should give what he has decided in his heart to give, not reluctantly or under compulsion, for God loves a cheerful giver." Pass the coin around again. Eventually, the coin should land in the hands of someone you have "planted" in the group to use as part of the game. This person will have been instructed in advance NOT to pass the button on to someone else. So, when you ask who has the button and everyone has had a chance to guess, this person will still have the button. Remind him or her of the rules of the game and repeat the exercise. During this second pass, he or she will fail to pass along the button again and you will have to remove the child from the game. Share the passage in Luke 6:38, "Give and it will be given to you. A good measure, pressed down, shaken together and running over, will be poured into your lap. For with the measure you use, it will be measured to you." After you have made your point, let the kids know that your "plant" was part of the game all along and was helping teach them an important lesson. If the kids enjoyed the game, play a few more rounds.)

Dramatizations

Have you ever gone to the movies to see a story that you first read in a book? If the filmmaker has done his or her homework, it can be one of life's great pleasures. I can think of no better example of this than a recent trip to the Cineplex. The movie *How the Grinch Stole Christmas* is based on the famous book by Dr. Seuss. I grew up reading that book and watching the animated tale every Christmas. I even had a stuffed Grinch! Imagine my delight at seeing my old friend on the big screen. Despite the reviews, I was totally captivated and completely engrossed by the portrayal of the character. I even appreciated the back-story and subplots that were not part of the book. It was as if I were visiting a very old friend and finding out new things about him that I didn't know. A dramatic portrayal of a biblical character can be just as exciting for a child (of any age!). Whether it is a fictional character like the lost sheep in one of Jesus' parables or a more well known character like Lazarus or Moses, it's always fun to "see" the people we are reading about and get to know them in another dimension. Now, before you skip this section because you don't think you're an actor or actress, or you think it will take too much time to memorize lines, consider these ideas:

- **Use puppets.** With or without a puppet stage, elaborate puppets, or even exceptional puppetry skills, you can make this work! Children are eager to use their imagination if you have something to show them when you tell the story. I recently saw an artist do a brilliant program using marionettes. The puppeteer was in full view, but I was fully captivated by the visualization of his story. Ventriloquists and some puppeteers are in full view when they use their characters. We are willing to suspend belief and use our imagination to see and hear a good story.
- **Costuming.** This can be as simple as a hat or cloak or even a prop. For example, you can become Queen Esther with a crown or Ruth with a shawl. David can be played with a slingshot and shepherd's headpiece. In other words, just the "suggestion" of another character through costume or prop is sufficient.
- **Readers theatre.** If you are familiar with the script, you can read it while you act out the character. This is not a license to read it to the children. You must "act it out" while you read it. Again, it's the visualization of the battle, the chase scene, or even the love story that will make it interesting.

The Lost Sheep

Scripture: "Each one is tempted when, by his own evil desire, he is dragged away and enticed. Then, after desire has conceived, it gives birth to sin; and sin, when it is full-grown, gives birth to death" (James 1:14-15).

Theme: Going "our own way" and doing "our own thing" is often a dangerous option.

Character: A teenage girl on the run. She's dressed in "sheep's clothing," which should be some type of cape or woolly-looking jacket and a hood with sheep ears. A prosthetic nose and/or makeup is also an option. She's trendy, pretty, and popular.

[Note: You will also need a few offstage voices to help with the "howling."]

Setting: Anywhere.

(As the scene begins the SHEEP enters at a brisk pace, takes a couple of glances over her shoulder as if to see if anyone is following her, pauses, and finally strikes a more relaxed pose. As she begins to speak, she flips her hair or the hood of her "costume" back and fluffs her hair. Perhaps she has a little makeup kit stashed away inside the garment or in a purse that can be hanging over her shoulder.)

SHEEP: Excuse me? Do you happen to know the way to the mall? I'm just a little lost here . . . not like a "lost sheep" or anything. We're not all shy, stupid, stubborn, and lost. Whatever! That whole flock thing is so overrated anyway. And a shepherd? Hmmph. I don't think so. Like I'm some kind of animal that needs to be pushed to get around. You can just keep your rod and staff, thank you. Just point me in the general direction of the Galleria, and I can get there myself. (Waving behind her) Good-bye, green pastures and still, quiet waters. I am headed to the Bistro and Body Shop, thank you very much. First stop, makeup! (Looking at arm) Ol' Shep thought it would be cute if all of his "property" had tattoos. Sha, right! Tattoos are so not fixable. It's a wonder a sheep like me can maintain her individuality at all. Shepherds are so clueless, don't you think? They just don't get it. It's so easy for them . . . roll out of bed, put on a bedouin cap . . . backward, and head for the fridge. Animals! (Looking at fingernails) Just look at these stems. I practically broke a hoof here. (Looking at coat/costume) And my wool!

This is going to take a total makeover: manicure, makeup, grooming, the works. Shopping relieves stress, don't you think? If you were a sheep like me, you would totally understand these things.

(Rising, moves toward the direction of entrance, sighs) They'll miss me back there. I was practically the queen of fashion for the flock. They'll be left a vast wasteland of the ensembly challenged. A flock of clones: Dollys everywhere. Their flock stock will totally drop, a shameless spiral. (Returns to chair and sits) But it was time. Ol' Shep's attitude had gotten so bad. So many rules. As if! Like the other day we're out in the field doing the grazing thing, right, and I spot this little oasis of green grass. Being the furiously independent ewe that I am, I head to the fence line, look for a hole, and I'm outtie. Well, almost outtie, 'til Ol' Shep grabs me by the *hind quarters* and pulls me back under the fence. *(Stops abruptly)* How totally rude. Then he starts with the speech. "Miss Gadabout" . . . Miss Gadabout? How Jurassic is that? "Miss Gadabout. You stray from the flock like a sheep without a shepherd. Stay close lest you become a sheep among the wolves. My sheep know my voice and they obey." Oooooooh.

(If glasses have been removed, put them back on and stand as if to leave.) Well, it's getting late and I'm sure that Ol' Shep is looking for me by now. He's so furiously overprotective. So, if you'll just point toward the mall?

(The sound of howling wolves or a howling wolf is heard offstage. I have also used the theme music to the movie "Jaws." Notice the sounds, but act unafraid.)

My advice? Stay away from the croutons at McDonalds. I hear they are breaded time bombs. *(Sound of howling persists, getting a little stronger/closer.)*

I'm not afraid of lions or tigers or . . . *(As the sound intensifies, become noticeably nervous.)* Maybe this wasn't such a good idea. Shep? Oh, what was that thing you said? "Even though I walk through the valley of the shadow of death, I will fear no evil." Maybe this wasn't such a good idea after all. Shep? Shep? *(Starts to wander off the stage and begins bleating as the sound of the wolves or the theme music intensifies)*

Lazarus

Scripture: "I want to know Christ and the power of his resurrection and the fellowship of sharing in his sufferings, becoming like him in his death" (Philippians 3:10).

Theme: The resurrection power of Christ

Character: Traditional biblical character

Setting: A back street in Jerusalem shortly after the Resurrection

(LAZARUS *enters with back to the audience. He is dressed in biblical garb to include a headpiece, used to help keep his face partially hidden. He slowly whistles, "Christ the Lord Is Risen Today." He moves slowly and methodically across the back of the stage, still keeping his back to the audience, trying not to be too conspicuous. Once he has crossed the stage, he turns his head over his shoulder and toward the audience. He is wearing Groucho Marx glasses. This needs to momentarily register with the audience before he moves again. He continues to whistle and takes a seat on a "bench" placed downstage. He can also carry a cloth bag filled with some type of seed that he uses to feed the birds in the city. He sits on the bench and opens the bag to feed the birds. After glancing left and right again. He stops whistling and addresses the "person" standing near him. Most of what he says is spoken in a stage whisper.*)

LAZARUS: Pssst. Over here. It's me, Lazarus. *(Pause)* Of course, *the* Lazarus. How many guys do you know with the name Lazarus? *(Beat)* What do you think of the disguise? *(Nods)* It was Mary's idea. She's so dramatic. She thought it would help me blend in. *(Looks around again)* The place is crawlin' with religious people. It gives me the creeps. But I had to find you. Have you heard the news? *(Pause)* Jesus is alive. *(Trying to quiet listener)* Keep it down! You're going to blow my cover, here. *(Pause)* No, I haven't seen Him. In case you've forgotten, I'm hiding. They're tryin' to kill me, remember? Ever since Jesus raised me from the dead, they think I'm part of a secret plot. *(Pause)* Oh, you think I'm crazy? *(Beat)* They killed Jesus, didn't they? *(Beat, smirk)* Well, they tried. Now they're trying to kill anyone who had anything to do with His ministry. They want to strike while the fire's hot, I suppose.

(Beat) Word is that Mary saw Him early this morning. *(Pause)* No, not my sister, Mary. Mary Magdalene. *(Pause)* Why not her? She was the only one looking for Him, wasn't she? Which is more than I can say for them other chickens that flew the coop. *(Beat)* Like I should talk, hidin' behind this getup.

(Beat) It doesn't matter if she saw Him or not. He's alive, I'm tellin' ya. *(Pause)* How do I know? *(Louder)* How do I . . . ? *(Stops, hides face momentarily to escape unwanted attention)* Don't get me all riled up like that. *(Beat)* How do I know? I *know* the power of His resurrection. In case

you're forgettin', I was dead. I know what it means to die and be absent from the body. For three days, I rested in Abraham's bosom while my flesh rotted in a tomb. Then came the sound of His voice calling my name . . . *(Beat)* "Lazarus." Just the sound of His voice broke the chains of death. Oh, He's alive, all right. Let's see . . . *(Thinking)* What day is today? The first day of the week, right? That's *(counting)* three days. Oh yeah, He's alive. I know it here. *(Points to heart)* They might have killed His body, but they'll never silence His voice. Never!

    (Stands to leave) You've got to go and tell the others that what Mary is saying is the truth. *(Pause)* Me? I'll bide my time until I can shout it from the rooftops . . . no, from the mountaintops! *(Getting louder)* Jesus is . . . *(Catches himself, lets voice fall to a whisper as he looks nervously from side to side)* He's alive. *(Beat)* I've got to go. Martha will be frantic. She's such a blessing to me, but she's going to send me to an early grave . . . again. *(Starts to slowly whistle "Christ the Lord Is Risen Today" walking US. Just before he turns his back to the audience, he pulls the glasses down over his nose, winks, and nods. Picks up step, exits whistling.)*

Have You Seen My Ruler?

Scripture: "So that Christ may dwell in your hearts through faith" (Ephesians 3:17).

Theme: God lives in the hearts of believers.

Characters:
MOSES: Traditional
BEZALEL: Construction foreman
OHOLIAB: Construction worker

Setting: Workstation. The sounds of hammers and saws and other related building construction sounds are heard.

MOSES: Hi, kids! Just got back from a little trip to the mountains where God told me an amazing thing. Excuse me . . . Hey, can you guys keep the noise down a little?

BEZALEL *(offstage voice):* Sorry.

MOSES: As I was saying, we're building a home for God. We're pretty excited down here. The ruler of heaven and earth to dwell among men.

BEZALEL *(enters):* Ruler? Have you seen one? I lost mine.

MOSES: Hi, Bezzy. This is Bezalel, kids. He's one of the master craftsmen in charge of this project. God said to pick only the best for this building.

BEZALEL: By the way, what's a cubit?

MOSES: Ask Oholiab. (BEZALEL *exits.*) As I was saying, can you imagine sharing your house with God? Matter of fact, the guys are working on it already. *(Pulls out blueprint)* See, this place, right here? *(Points to area called holy of holies)* That's *His* room. It's called the holy of holies. Between you and me, it doesn't seem big enough for God. But He was very specific about the size. There's no closet space at all. I don't know where He's going to hang His robes.

OHOLIB *(offstage voice):* Anyone seen the plane?

BEZALEL *(offstage voice):* It's at the airport.

MOSES: Is this really the best we could do? Anyway, God was very specific about everything. Yo, Oh, come up and say hello!

OHOLIAB *(enters):* Sorry, Mo. Can't talk now. We've got a problem.

MOSES: What's the matter?

OHOLIAB: Well, you know that big announcement you made about people bringing freewill offerings for this place?

MOSES: Yeah.

OHOLIAB: We have enough acacia wood outside to build 10 of these babies. You got to tell them to stop.

MOSES: I'll take care of it at the meeting tonight.

OHOLIAB: Thanks. *(Exits)*

MOSES: Great craftsman, but he tends to get a little stressed out.

BEZALEL: It's a miracle! It's a miracle!

MOSES: What happened?

BEZALEL: It's Sheba, the blind carpenter. He picked up his hammer and saw! *(Exits)*

MOSES *(shakes his head)*: Anyway, it's going to be the nicest place in town. It should be, don't you think? I mean it *is* the place where God is going to live. And *He* should have only the best, right? *(All building sounds stop.)*

MOSES: Hey, what's going on down there?

OHOLIAB *(enters with* BEZALEL, *holding another blueprint)*: Uh, Mo, do you know anything about this being a temporary building?

MOSES: Temporary?

OHOLIAB: Yeah, like God might not stay here very long?

MOSES: Well, I can't be speaking for God, but I don't know any other place that would be nicer than this place.

BEZALEL: Some of the guys were talking. They were just wondering how a building like this could hold God. You know, Him bein' so big and all.

OHOLIAB: You know, just wondering, that's all. (BEZALEL *and* OHOLIAB *exit.)*

MOSES *(to kids)*: Can you think of a place where God could live that would be nicer than the Tabernacle? I mean, according to these plans, I suppose He doesn't need a lot of room. But, it would have to be a very, very special place. Where would He go?

(MOSES encourages children to talk about God coming to live in their hearts through the Holy Spirit.)

BEZALEL *(offstage voice)*: Did someone order two golden chairs for God's room?

OHOLIAB *(offstage voice)*: Not chairs! Cherubs. Send them back to the black-smiths and tell them to get it right.

MOSES: Well, I have to get to that meeting about the acacia wood. *(Begins to depart)* Hey, maybe this could be the first *board* meeting.

Interactive Storytelling

Interactive storytelling is one of my favorite ways to communicate the gospel. Anytime you can get children involved in the process of telling a story, you have greatly increased your chances of getting them to remember it. The process of interacting with the children creates a virtual learning center that makes the process fun and memorable. These next four ideas make use of cuing an audience response through signs, gestures, and words. Some, like "Jesus in the Boat," are more active than others, but all of them will get the children involved. Parables are especially effective stories to use. Any story in the Bible that insinuates movement is material that can be considered. You may also want to consider asking some questions about the content of the story when you are through to reinforce the point of the story.

Abraham and Isaac

(Read Genesis 22:1-14. This is a simple audience participation story that uses cue cards for prompting. The signs should read: "Yo!" "Ahhh," "Oh no!" "Cheer," "Animal Sounds." They should be easily readable. The audience should be instructed that the "Animal Sounds" is the sound of whatever animal is read in context [i.e., sheep, donkey, etc.]. A person from the audience can be in charge of the cue cards, but the piece works better if the NARRATOR also manages the cue cards. Additional cues can be given by hand signals. Assign a series of hand signals to each word and prompt the audience with a gesture. For example, pumping your fist once could be the cue for "Yo!" and placing your hand over your heart and patting your chest with the open palm could be the cue for "Ahhh.")

NARRATOR: Once there was a man named Abraham. *[Cheer]* God blessed Abraham in his old age with a son named Isaac, whom he loved very much. *["Ahhh"]* One day God said to Abraham *["Yo!"]*. Abraham replied *["Yo!"]*. Then God said, "Take your son, your only son, Isaac, whom you love very much *["Ahhh"]* and go north to Mount Moriah. There you will sacrifice him as a burnt offering on one of the mountains. *["Oh no!"]*

Early the next morning, Abraham got up and saddled his donkey. *[Animal Sounds]* He left for Mount Moriah with two of his servants and his son, Isaac, whom he loved very much. *["Ahhh"]* On the third day, Abraham looked up and saw the mountains in the distance. He said to his servants *["Yo!"]*, "Stay here and look after the donkey. *[Animal Sounds]* I will take the boy to the mountain and we will offer a sacrifice." *["Oh no!"]*

Abraham took the wood for the burnt offering and gave it to Isaac, whom he loved very much. *["Ahhh"]* He himself took the knife. *["Oh no!"]* As the two of them walked along, Isaac said to his father *["Yo!"]*, "I see the fire and the wood are here, but where is the lamb?" *[Animal Sounds]* Abraham replied *["Yo!"]*, "God will provide the lamb." *[Animal Sounds]* And so they went on together to Mount Moriah.

Finally they arrived at the location. *[Cheer]* Then Abraham took his son, Isaac, whom he loved very much, *["Ahhh"]* and bound him and laid him on top of the altar. *["Oh no!"]* He took the knife out of his pocket *["Oh no!"]* and lifted it over top of the boy *["Oh no!"]* to kill him. *["OH NO!"]* *(Note: Try to encourage the preceding set of "Oh no" responses to get louder each time.)* Just at that very moment an angel called out to Abraham from heaven. *["Yo!"]* Abraham replied. *["Yo!"]* The angel said, "Don't lay a hand on the boy. *[Cheer]* Now I know that you fear God, because you have not withheld even your son, Isaac, whom you love very much. *["Ahhh"]*

Abraham looked up and there in a thicket was a lamb *[Animal Sounds]* caught in the bushes. He went over and took the lamb *[Animal Sounds]* and sacrificed it as a burnt offering to the Lord instead of his own son. *[Cheer]* And Abraham named God Jehovah Jireh that day because God had provided a lamb. *[Animal Sounds]*

Questions:

- Who told Abraham to go to Mount Moriah? (God)
- Did Abraham obey God? (Yes. He took his son to Mount Moriah to sacrifice him according to what he had been told.)
- How did God know that Abraham loved him? (He obeyed God.)
- What animal did God use as a sacrifice? (A ram in the thicket)

The Parable of the Talents

(Read Matthew 25:14-30. The following parable utilizes children's musical instruments such as whistles, kazoos, party horns, and so forth, to tell the story.)

STUDENT 1: Kazoo—plays sound of trumpet announcing arrival of a king or other royalty

STUDENT 2: Toy xylophone with a full musical scale on it—plays eight notes

STUDENT 3: Slide whistle

STUDENT 4: Whistle

STUDENT 5: Rattle or maraca

STUDENT 6: Party horn

STUDENT 7: Kazoo—plays "For He's a Jolly Good Fellow"

STUDENT 8: Kazoo—plays a death dirge

(STUDENTS should be instructed to play "responses" on demand. This can be accomplished by pointing to the STUDENT or some other sort of visual cuing. As an option to the story, four other STUDENTS can act out the story [KING, SERVANT 1, SERVANT 2, SERVANT 3]. Their actions should be large pantomime. If clown costuming and/or makeup are available, it will enhance the storytelling. STUDENTS can also double up on several instruments.)

*NOTE: I recommend that Student 2 be an older youth or adult.

NARRATOR: Once there was a king. (STUDENT 1) A king who had many talents. (STUDENT 2 *goes up the scale once.*) One day the king decided to go on an exciting journey. (STUDENT 5) So he called for his servants to divide up his property. (STUDENT 4) To the first servant he gave five talents. (STUDENT 2 *plays the first five notes of the scale.*) To the second servant he gave two talents. (STUDENT 2 *plays the sixth and seventh notes of the scale.*) And to the third servant he gave one talent. (STUDENT 2 *plays the eighth note of the scale.*) And then the king (STUDENT 1) departed for his exciting journey. (STUDENT 5) The first servant went out and began to use what had been given him to make others happy. (STUDENT 2 *plays the first five notes of the scale going up and down about three times.*) Likewise, the second servant went out and began to use what had been given him to make others happy. (STUDENT 2 *plays the A and B notes back and forth about four times.*) But the third servant was mad that he had only been given one note to play. (STUDENT 2 *plays the high C note once.*) So he went out and had a party. (STUDENT 6) After a long time the king (STUDENT 1) returned from his exotic journey (STUDENT 5). He called for his servants to give an account. (STUDENT 4) The three servants came back with this account. (STUDENT 2 *uses the xylophone to play "Do-Re-Mi" from the musical* The Sound of Music.

[This may sound like a task, but it is really quite easy to play with a toy xylophone. Don't abandon the story at this point! It doesn't have to sound perfect. The important thing is that the very last note of the song, "Do-Re-Mi" needs to be the sound of the party horn from STUDENT 6 *instead of the assigned C note played by* STUDENT 2!] *You might repeat the last phrase with the party horn at the very end to accentuate the point that the third servant didn't use his note to make others happy.)* To the first servant, the king responded . . . (STUDENT 7) To the second servant the king responded . . . (STUDENT 7) But to the third servant the king said . . . (STUDENT 8) And then the king called for his guards. (STUDENT 4) He commanded his guards to take that wicked and lazy servant and throw him out into the outer darkness where there would be no happy sounds. (STUDENT 6) For everyone who has and uses what he or she has to serve others, even more will be given. But from everyone who doesn't have and doesn't use what he or she is given to serve others, even what little he or she has will be taken away. Let those who have ears to hear . . . *(All make a noise with their instruments at the same time.)*

Questions:
- What did the king do with his money (talents) when he went away? (He gave it to his servants.)
- What did the first two servants do with the king's money? (They went out and invested the money so the king received back double what he gave to them.)
- What did the third servant do with the king's money? (He buried it so that no one would steal it.)
- When the king returned, what did he do with the third servant? (He threw him outside and gave his talent to another servant.)

The Body of Christ Is an Ocean

(This storytelling technique incorporates the text of 1 Corinthians 12:12-27 and involves audience participation through word cues. Divide your group into six equal units and assign each group a fish in the ocean. Explain to them that when the NARRATOR says their word cue in the story, they should stand up and respond as a group.)

Responses:

ANGELFISH: Repeatedly flap your arms like an angel.

CRABFISH: Snap your fingers.

BLOWFISH: Blow throw pursed lips like trying to blow a bubble without the gum.

JELLYFISH: Shake all over.

SHARKS: Extend both arms forward, fully extended at the elbow and bring the hands together moving up and down to simulate the jaws of the shark biting down on something.

(When movements have been assigned, tell the entire group that every time the NARRATOR uses the word "Ocean" they are to do the wave . . . as a large group . . . from left to right and then back from right to left. Allow each group enough time respond to their cue before moving on in the story.)

NARRATOR: The Body of Christ is an **Ocean,** although it is made up of different fish: **Sharks, Angelfish, Blowfish, Crabs, and Jellyfish.** And although the fish are many, they form one **Ocean.** If the **Jellyfish** should say, "Because I am not a **Shark,** I am not a part of the **Ocean,"** it is not for that reason any less a part of it. And if the **Angelfish** should say, "Because I am not a **Crab,** I am not a part of the **Ocean,"** it is not for that reason any less a part of it. If the whole **Ocean** were filled with **Blowfish,** where would all the **Sharks** be? If the whole **Ocean** were filled with **Jellyfish,** where would all the **Crabs** be? But, in fact, God has arranged the fish just as he wanted them to be. The **Angelfish** cannot say to the **Blowfish,** "I don't need you." Likewise, the **Crabs** cannot say to the **Jellyfish,** "I don't need you." Now you are a part of the **Ocean** and each one of you is a fish in it.

Questions:
- Who is the "Body of Christ" in this passage of scripture? (People in the church.)
- How does this passage of the Bible tell us to treat each other? (We must respect each other and work together.)
- Is one person in God's family more important than another? (We are all equal in God's eyes.)
- Why do you think God makes us different? (We all have different jobs to do.)

Jesus in the Boat

(Read Mark 4:35-41. This story can be told with as few as four children and as many as you can handle. I recommend it for middle school children. Divide the audience into three groups: WIND, WAVE, *and* THUNDER. *Select several individuals to participate as the* DISCIPLES. *Place the* DISCIPLES *on the stage or in front of the audience.)*

Responses:

WIND: "And the **Wind** blew." *(Everyone in the "Wind" section of the audience will stand up and wave their arms over their heads left to right. Additionally, they will make "wind sounds.")*

WAVE: "And the **Waves** beat against the boat." *(The "Waves" will stand up and lift their arms in front of them above their heads and then back to their sides. Additionally, they will all say, "Whoosh.")*

THUNDER: "And the **Thunder** roared." *(The "Thunder" section of the audience will stand and flex their arms to show their muscles. They will all say, "Grrrrrr.")*

DISCIPLES: "Lighten the load," "Row! Row!" "All hands on deck." *(The* DISCIPLES *also respond to a series of audio cues from the* NARRATOR. *On the first cue,* **"Lighten the load,"** *all the* DISCIPLES *throw their hands up in the air and yell, "Wheee." On* **"Row! Row!"** *the* DISCIPLES *sit on the floor and pantomime a rowing motion. When the* NARRATOR *shouts,* **"All hands on deck"** *the* DISCIPLES *should drop to their hands and knees. Additionally, the* DISCIPLES *should be advised to follow any other cues the* NARRATOR *might read in the story.*

(Once all the cues and responses have been established, you should advise the audience and the DISCIPLES *that when you say the word* **"Storm"** *everyone in the audience should do their motions together. On the word* **"Storm"** *the* DISCIPLES *should cry out "Help!" Lastly, you should direct one person in the very center of the audience to be* **Jesus.** *This person should be directed to say* **"Peace, be still"** *whenever called upon. Once* NARRATOR *has made all the appropriate assignments and practiced all the parts [each group should practice their cues before beginning the story] you're ready to begin the narration.)*

NARRATOR: Leaving the crowd behind, the disciples took Jesus along, just as He was, in the boat. There were also other boats with Him. Suddenly, a squall came upon them. The **Wind** began to blow. Peter shouted, **"All hands on deck."** The **Waves** crashed against the boat. Peter called out to the disciples, **"Lighten the load."** Dark, angry clouds, filled the sky and **Thunder** began to roar. Peter commanded his little group, **"Row! Row!"** It was a terrible **Storm.**

  The **Wind** began to blow harder. The **Waves** beat against the tiny fishing boat. The **Thunder** continued to roar. Peter needed more help.

"All hands on deck," he bellowed. But the **Storm** was relentless. The disciples threw more things overboard. **"Lighten the load,"** they yelled to one another. Still the **Storm** persisted. They tried to push through. **"Row! Row!"** But the **Storm** was too much.

Throughout the night the disciples fought the ferocious weather. **Thunder . . . Waves . . . Wind . . . Waves . . . Thunder . . .** (NARRATOR *can have a little fun with this section without wearing it out.*)

The disciples tried everything. **"Lighten the load" . . . "Row! Row!" . . . "All hands on deck" . . . "Row! Row!" . . . "All hands on deck"** (NARRATOR *can again have a little fun here, but don't wear it out!*) But nothing worked. It was the **Storm** to end all **Storms.** Finally, the disciples called for Jesus.

And Jesus rose up and said, **"Peace, be still."** [Note: If JESUS stands up and delivers his line without your prompt, continue on.] Immediately, the **Wind** ceased to blow. The **Waves** stopped pounding the side of the tiny boat. The **Thunder** roared no more.

The disciples were terrified and asked each other, "Who is this? Even the wind and the waves obey him!" (Mark 4:41).

Questions:
- What happened to the disciples? (They were in a boat on the Sea of Galilee and a storm came upon them.)
- Were the disciples afraid? (Yes, they thought they were going to drown.)
- Where was Jesus? (He was asleep in the stern of the ship.)
- What did Jesus do? (He commanded the storm to stop.)

Visualizing Activities

A director of a play should never stage a scene without knowing the details of the setting. Props, costumes, and set pieces are a small part of the grand scheme of things in a play but should be strategically and deliberately placed and used in order to add texture to the text of a play. As a teacher, you don't need to understand the dynamics of a theatrical production to appreciate the idea that context is important to a story. Visualizing scenes in the Bible will require you to go past the text and into the context. Consider the story of the woman caught in the act of adultery in John 8. This is a gripping tale of human drama. It represents the intersection of law, culture, geography, history, commerce, religion, politics, and a myriad of other aspects of life. They all collide in 11 verses in chapter 8. How then do you visualize the moment in time when the woman is thrown at the feet of Jesus? It involves countless decisions based on a wealth of information that bring us to that time and place in history. I'm certainly overstating my case here, but the idea that every story has dimension is important. These next three ideas use tableau, pantomime, and dowel rods to help the pictures of the Bible pop off the page.

The Parable of the Sower

(Read Matthew 13:3-9. Tableaus are like freeze-frames on a video. Another way to consider a tableau is like a picture. By putting several of these "living pictures" together, you can create a "slide show" that will help your children visualize the story. As a storytelling technique, use a convention with the eyelids called, "Curtain up/Curtain down." Explain to the audience that when the NARRATOR says, "Curtain down," people should close their eyes. This will allow your players time to get into position while the NARRATOR speaks. At the appropriate moment in the script the NARRATOR should say, "Curtain up," to let the audience know it's time to look at the picture. Allow the audience about four seconds to take in the picture before having them return to "Curtain down." There should be no movement onstage while the audience has their eyes open.)

Characters:

> FARMER
> SEED 1
> SEED 2
> SEED 3
> SEED 4
> 2 BIRDS
> SUN
> 2 THORNS

NARRATOR: The parable of the sower.

(Curtain down)

> **[Picture 1**—FARMER *and four* SEEDS *gather together for a group picture.]*

NARRATOR: Then Jesus told many parables about the kingdom of God. This is the story about a farmer, who went out to sow his seeds.

(Curtain up. Pause. Curtain down.)

> **[Picture 2**—FARMER *and* SEEDS *(2, 3, 4) move SL leaving* SEED 1 *alone on SR.* TWO BIRDS *are picking at* SEED 1 *and the* SEED *appears to cry out for help.]*

NARRATOR: As he was scattering the seed, some fell along the path and the birds came and ate it up.

(Curtain up. Pause. Curtain down.)

> **[Picture 3**—SEED 1 *exits.* SEED 2 *moves to SL as if being left behind the others still "sowing" SR.* SEED 2 *appears to be happily growing up and sprouting new and tender shoots.]*

NARRATOR: Some fell on rocky places where it did not have much soil. It sprang up quickly, because the soil was shallow.

(Curtain up. Pause. Curtain down.)

[**Picture 4**—SEED 2 *withers while* SUN *gives a menacing glare from somewhere behind* SEED 2.]

NARRATOR: But when the sun came up, the plants were scorched, and they withered because they had no root.

(Curtain up. Pause. Curtain down.)

[**Picture 5**—SEED 2 *exits.* SEED 3 *moves SL as if being left behind by* FARMER *and* SEED 4 *on SR.* SEED 3 *is being choked by* TWO THORNS.]

NARRATOR: Other seeds fell among the thorns, who grew up and choked the plants.

(Curtain up. Pause. Curtain down.)

[**Picture 6**—SEED 3 *exits.* SEED 4 *moves to CS and poses like a weightlifter or body builder flexing his or her muscles.* FARMER *admires from the side. You might also consider having the* SUN, BIRDS, *and* THORNS *watching from a distance and posed to show their fear of this* SEED.]

NARRATOR: Still other seed fell on good soil where it produced a crop—100, 60, or 30 times what was sown.

(Curtain up. Pause. Curtain down.)

[**Picture 7**—ALL *the players form a line across the stage facing the audience.]*

NARRATOR: He that has ears to hear, let him hear.

(Curtain up)

[**Picture 8**—EVERYONE *takes a bow.]*

The Story of Creation

 (Read Genesis 1. This visualization technique uses dowel rods to interpret text by creating and forming abstract pictures. The dowel rods should be ³/₈" in diameter and 3' in length. Begin by holding one dowel rod in each hand along each side of your body, at the seam of your pants. "Choke up" on the stick until it rests about 2" off the floor. We'll refer to this position henceforth as the "neutral position." The NARRATOR should read the line followed by the dowel movement. The NARRATOR may also do the interpretation.)

NARRATOR: In the beginning, there was nothing but God.

(Place the dowel in the form of an "X," with the intersection of the "X" just below the face. Henceforth, we'll refer to this position as the "X' position.")

 NARRATOR: And God said let there be light.

(Lift the dowel rods above the head, parallel to each other but perpendicular to the floor. Then move them away from each other and back to the "neutral position.")

NARRATOR: And it was good.

(Return to the "X' position.")

NARRATOR: On the second day . . .

(Tap the dowel rods twice in the "X' position." Move sticks parallel to the ground. [Henceforth, tap the dowels together to signify the number of the day; that is, tap three times for "on the third day," etc.])

 NARRATOR: God created the heavens . . .

(Place the dowels at face level, parallel to the floor. [Henceforth, we'll refer to this position as the "level position."] Elevate the upper dowel rod 6" from its starting point.)

NARRATOR: . . . and the earth.

(Lower the bottom dowel rod 6" from its starting point.)

NARRATOR: And it was good.

(Return to the "X' position.")

NARRATOR: On the third day *(Tap three times. Move sticks parallel to the ground.)*, God gathered the waters together . . .

(Move to the "level position." Move the upper dowel to a position 6" to the right of its current position. Roll the wrist as you move the dowel to create the idea of a wave on the water.)

NARRATOR: . . . and dry land appeared.

 (Drop the head to look directly at the lower dowel rod. Nod your head.)

NARRATOR: And it was good.

(Return to the "'X' position.")

NARRATOR: On the fourth day . . .

(Tap the sticks together four times and immediately return to the "neutral position.")

NARRATOR: God made the sun to shine during the day . . .

 (From the "neutral position," move the dowels away from the center of the body and up until the ends of the dowel rods touch each other directly over your head. With the sticks traveling away from the body in both directions, it should make the appearance as if you are drawing a big circle to represent the sun.)

NARRATOR: . . . and the stars to shine at night.

 (Tap the ends of the dowels together like the twinkling of a star to a place below and to the right of where the sticks connected when drawing the sun. [Note: Only tap the ends of the dowels.])

NARRATOR: And it was good.

(Return to the "'X' position.")

NARRATOR: On the fifth day . . .

(Tap the dowels together five times and immediately move to the "level position." At this point, we'll make some small modifications to this position. In the "level position" indicated above, the dowels are grasped with the palms facing toward the floor. Take the bottom dowel and hold it with the palm facing up. Then tilt the right *side of the top dowel downward and the right side of the lower dowel upward so that they cross somewhere up to 7" to 12" from the right side of the dowel rods [as you look upon them]. Think of the picture you've just created as a giant pair of hedge clippers.)*

NARRATOR: God filled the seas with fish . . .

(To "move" the fish through the water, just start "clipping the hedges" from left to right. In conjunction with the text, this action will create the imagery of "flaring" fish gills as the fish moves through water.)

NARRATOR: And put the birds in the air.

(Change the direction of the "fish movement" to the left and move the intersection of the dowels toward the middle of each stick. Tilt the dowel rods upward and make *the same "cutting motion" as the dowels fly upward and away to the left like a bird flapping its wings and flying upward. [Note: At the end of your arm extension, you may want to pantomime the idea that something fell out of the air and landed on your face. You can wipe this off with your sleeve and shake your head in disgust.])*

NARRATOR: And it was good.

(Return to the "'X' position.")

NARRATOR: On the sixth day . . .

(Tap the sticks six times and go to "neutral position.")

NARRATOR: God made the animals. He made the rhino.

(Make a fist around the end of the dowel in your right hand and then place the fist on your forehead, so that the dowel rod sticks up and out of your head like a horn on a unicorn. Make a fist around the end of the *dowel in your left hand and then place it behind you so that it "wags" like a tail.)*

NARRATOR: He made the elephant.

 (Same idea as the previous one, except that you move the right hand that is on the forehead to the nose and point the stick downward. The other stick returns to neutral. [Note: Consider tilting the head upward and lifting the end of the stick up in the air, while holding it firmly on the nose.])

 NARRATOR: He made the giraffe.

(Stand one dowel on the ground and the other upon it as if building a line to the sky. Use the left hand to connect the dowels and the right hand to work the head of the giraffe like it were the head of a puppet. [Note: You can create other animals with the dowel rods and extend this part of the story.])

NARRATOR: He made the alligator.

(Two sticks opening and closing at the mouth)

NARRATOR: And it was good.

(Return to the "'X' position.")

NARRATOR: Also on the sixth day . . .

(Tap the dowels together six times and then move the dowel directly in front of you so that they make the picture of a "T." The dowel in your left hand should be the crossbar.)

NARRATOR: God decided to create a helper. So He made man from the ground by blowing life into him.

(Move the dowel in the right hand, the upright stick, up and "through" the crossbar of the "T" as if it was a plant pushing its way through the ground level, while holding the crossbar in place. Continue to move it until the bottom of the dowel in the right hand is almost level with the crossbar. Then wiggle it as if to show that it is alive. [Note: Precipitate this movement by blowing on the dowel rod when the text says, "blowing life".])

NARRATOR: And that was very good.

Then God said, "It is not good for man to be alone." So He made a helper for man. He put the man into a deep sleep.

(Take the upright bar, the one of movement in the previous interpretation [right hand] and move the top of it toward the right to show weariness or leaning.)

NARRATOR: Then God took a rib from the man's side.

(Take the crossbar, the one that was stationary in the previous interpretation, and forcefully pull it away and to the left of the upright dowel rod. [Note: You may want to grimace and contract over the left hip as if to demonstrate the pain.])

NARRATOR: From the rib, He created woman.

(Move both dowel rods to an upright position [perpendicular to the floor] and parallel to each other, so they are side by side in front of you. There should be perhaps 6" to 8" between the parallel dowels.)

NARRATOR: God saw that all He had done was good and so on the seventh day, He rested.

(Slowly move the dowel rods into the "'X' position" and rest your head over top the intersection of the dowels as if sleeping.)

The Parable of the Good Samaritan

(Read Luke 10:30-36. The idea of moving pictures is also a great teaching tactic. Break up the story of the Good Samaritan into six scenes, as listed below, and assign each scene to a different student. The student must come up with one picture, pose, or action that best captures the essence of the scene and then repeat that action over and over until all the moving pictures are put together. Line up the students from left to right in a line. Instruct the students that they are to start their specific picture on your cue [which can be as simple as pointing to them or calling their name].) The rest of the students can then watch the story unfold as a "movie." Remember, once a student starts his or her move, he or she must repeat it until all the students are doing their individual moves together and the story is completed.)

NARRATOR: A man was going down to Jericho, when he fell into the hands of robbers who took everything he had and beat him up.

[Picture 1—Robber beating up the man.] (Pound fists on an imaginary door in front of you.)

NARRATOR: A priest saw the man but passed by on the other side of the road.

[Picture 2—Priest passing by the beat up man.] (Start with arms down to side, fold them across body and look away.)

NARRATOR: So, too, a Levite, when he came to the place and saw him, passed by on the other side.

[Picture 3—Levite passing by the beat up man.] (Start with arms down to side, fold them across body and look the other way.)

NARRATOR: But a Samaritan, as he traveled, came where the man was; and when he saw him, he took care of the man.

[Picture 4—Samaritan bandages up the man's wounds.] (Roll hand around arm in a circular motion as if wrapping in a bandage.)

NARRATOR: Then he put the man on his own donkey, took him to an inn, and took care of him.

[Picture 5—Samaritan carries the man to an inn.] (Note: I recommend two people on this picture. One is the Samaritan and the other is the man who has been robbed. The Samaritan should take the arm of the man and put it over his shoulders and behind his neck. The picture should be of them walking in place with the Samaritan holding up the man who has been robbed.)

NARRATOR: The next day he paid the innkeeper to look after him until he was well.

*[**Picture 6**—Samaritan pays the innkeeper to take care of him.] (Put hand into pocket and pretend to pull out a few coins, giving them to an imaginary person in front of you.)*